THE MESSENGER

UDC 141.339=111=03.161.1
BBC 87.7+86.4

THE MESSENGER /author-compiler: O.A. Ivanova.
– 2017. – 78 pages.

This book is dedicated to the Messenger of the Great White Brotherhood, Tatyana Nicholaevna Mickushina.

It contains articles, interviews, and quotes from public talks given by the Messenger in which she discusses her Mission on Earth, reveals the essence of the Teaching of the Masters of Wisdom, shares her experience on how to find God within oneself, and much more.

The article "Give Wings to a Soul," by the journalist L. Zitara from Latvia, discusses the life journey of T. N. Mickushina and her becoming the Messenger of the Great White Brotherhood.

UDC 141.339
BBC 87.7+86.4

Copyright © O.A. Ivanova, 2017
© T.N. Mickushina, 2017
All rights reserved.

ISBN-13: 978-1973908616
ISBN-10: 1973908611

Contents

Foreword 4

"This is my job — To Forgive and Love" 6

Inner consonance with God
by T. N. Mickushina 14

Give Wings to a Soul by L. Zitara 19

Internal and External Path
by T. N. Mickushina 46

From conversations with the Messenger 54

"I invite you to Labor Day!"
T. N. Mickushina's address to followers
of the Teaching of the Masters of Wisdom 65

We must return to God!
by O. A. Ivanova 69

Foreword

It is difficult to speak of an important, admirable person in such a way so as not to glorify, extoll, overpraise or create an idol, and all the more so because this is really no ordinary person, but rather, someone quite unique and extraordinary. For me this person is a Teacher who helps me to rewrite my life anew.

Tatyana Nicholaevna Mickushina.

On the one hand her name is known all over the world because her books are translated and read across 20 different languages. On the other hand, her name is scarcely known because as a rule, one who knows her wants to understand himself, why he lives on planet Earth, why society is as it is and how it can be made better.

The next immediate question is, "How does T. N. Mickushina know these things?"

She knows because she's the conductor of Universal, Cosmic, and Divine Knowledge on the Earth.

The people who read her books around the world with gratitude are absolutely sure of it.

Moreover, the people who read the books for quite a different purpose, or maybe don't read them at all but know of them through hearsay and try to fight against the author by the most crude and unsophisticated methods, are absolutely sure of it as well. Hence, they see her, and her books, as a real threat to their own well-being and their quiet well-fed world.

As it turns out, if you are satisfied with everything in this world, then perhaps you do not yet need to become acquainted with the Messenger of the Great White Brotherhood, Tatyana Nicholaevna Mickushina. Even though it's already late, her heart and the doors of the Teaching are always open to the seeker of Truth.

"This is my job — To Forgive and Love"

> I represent another country,
> which is on the subtle plane.
> *T. N. Mickushina*

The Messenger is the position

T. N. Mickushina is a part of the remarkable series of Messengers of the Great White Brotherhood. Helena Petrovna Blavatsky brought the first message to modern humanity. At the end of the XIX century, she brought back the knowledge of the Teachers of Mankind, the Mahatmas, the Masters of the Secret Brotherhood, the Lords of Shambhala, who, from the subtle planes of being, have guided humanity along the evolutionary Path for many millennia. The following Messengers of the Great White Brotherhood came after H. P. Blavatsky: in Russia, Helena Ivanovna and Nicholas Konstantinovich Roerich, who described in their books the work of the Brotherhood and the Spiritual Hierarchy; in America, Mark and Elizabeth Clare Prophet; and in Bulgaria, Peter Deunov and Omraam Mikhaël Aïvanhov. These are only the most well-known names of the Messengers.

And now, once again, we have a Messenger from Russia — Tatyana Nicholaevna Mickushina.

The understanding of one's mission comes to a person from the subtle plane, from the Divine world. Of course, it depends on the person himself how he perceives this instruction from Above.

"I am the Messenger of the Great White Brotherhood. The Great White Brotherhood represents the Lords of Shambhala, or the Ascended Masters, or the Teachers of Humanity, who came to planet Earth at the time of the Third Root Race. Prior to this They lived and taught among people. They then moved to the subtle plane, now residing in ethereal sacred Retreats and continuing from there to work with the humanity of the Earth. They are called the Great White Brotherhood.

"When I faced the question of what I should call myself, I asked the Masters. They told me: 'You are the Messenger of the Great White Brotherhood.' I explained to the Masters that we have a bad reputation with the Great White Brotherhood in Russia. To which I was told: 'This post is called - Messenger of the Great White Brotherhood.'

"This position is so called, and whoever says anything about me, well, that is the business of those who speak. Whoever makes a judgment about the Great White Brotherhood that is their own business. The Brotherhood does not gain or lose anything from it. I cannot adjust to every person. I serve the Masters, and what They want, I do. They want the title 'Messenger of the Great White Brotherhood' to be introduced this way, and They do not want to change the name of the Mantle for someone.

"I am not a Messenger for Russia. I am the Messenger of the Great White Brotherhood, and I represent the Masters on Earth. That is, in fact, like representing another country here, another country that is on the subtle plane."

"I'm just a match in the hands of God. But I won't trade my right to burn for anything"

In November 2002, the first issue of the electronic mailing "Sirius" was released, and in 2003, on the instructions of the Masters T. N. Mickushina created her website, calling it "Sirius." In her message to the readers of the site she wrote about the purpose of publishing online and her full responsibility for all the materials that are posted.

"Six months have passed since the first release of the "Sirius" mailing in November 2002. I looked through all the 39 issues released and tried to understand why I started this publication and what motivates me, forcing me to spend so much effort on each issue.

"And I understood the main purpose of my publication. **This is to contribute to what, in the end, the whole of mankind must come to — the restoration of our connection with God,**

not through an external teaching or ritual, but a direct inner connection with God. Most of the materials of "Sirius" somehow relate to this topic.

"Now I take responsibility before God and the people for the continuation of the mystical traditions in this edition underlying ancient and modern Teachings, obtained as a result of direct connection with God, including in the Essene community, the Pythagorean community, the works of Blavatsky, the Roerichs, and Mark and Elizabeth Prophet."

In 2004, T. N. Mickushina again confirms to the readers of the "Sirius" website that she continues to follow the chosen Path, speaking about her even greater responsibility for every word spoken and for each of her actions, which comes from the realization that she is a Messenger.

"What right do you think I have to teach? I do not know how I feel this right. I just cannot fail to do this.

"I can say that I confirm this right to teach prior to every release of "Sirius." Tests can be very difficult. This can be compared to swimming in a 5-6 point storm at sea. You just overcame the last wave, and the next one is covering your head; you completely lose your orientation: Where is the top, where is the bottom?

"Sometimes, when I'm preparing another edition of 'Sirius' I compare myself with a match, not with a torch, namely with a match. It flares up in the dark and lights something. I know what **the Path** is, some readers might imagine something else.

"But I will still burn. I'm just a match in the hands of God. And nothing more.

"But I will not change my right to burn for anything. And I will burn as long as God will allow me.

"This is my job — to Forgive and Love. So I resist terrorism, as well as any evil of this world.

"Any other thoughts, feelings, emotions (enmity, hatred, anger, condemnation, resentment) are capable of giving rise to other adverse consequences in this world of form (new acts of terrorism, wars, cataclysms).

"Someone must keep the Divine vibration. Keep the Flame. Keep Life. And do something."

Fifteen years have passed since the beginning of the creation of the "Sirius" website. Work on the site did not stop and does not stop for a single day. It has become even wider, larger, and at the same time deeper, more penetrating, more subtle.

This is the site of the Messenger of the Great White Brotherhood, and Divine Truth and Divine Wisdom flow through it into our world!"

T. N. Mickushina's address to the readers of the "Sirius" website

"The main part of the "Sirius" website represents the Messages, or Dictations that I have been receiving for 12 years, from 2005 to 2016.

"At the present time I have received over 480 Messages from more than 50 Beings of Light. These Beings are dwelling on the Higher Planes of Existence and are called upon to help mankind in their evolution. The Messages are given in the form of talks.

"The Messages altogether contain a harmonious Teaching, the basis of which is the Moral Law. The Beings of Light methodically explain and prove to the currently incarnated people why it is advantageous to adhere to moral principles in life. For this, knowledge of the two most important laws is given: the Law of Karma and the Law of Reincarnation.

"I have done everything in my power in order to receive the Messages. But in fact it was God Who did everything.

"With God!"
Tatyana Mickushina

That is a kind of higher goal that can be set and implemented by a person in his life: Serving God, Serving all people, serving Life.

And it may be the purpose and meaning of life for every human being.

"It is only necessary to live with God," says the Teacher, the Messenger of God Tatyana Mickushina.

And with great Love for each of us and with all the generosity of her spirit, she shares her understanding and experience of how we can approach and return to God.

Inner consonance with God
T. N. Mickushina

I will try to share with you my thoughts and my experience. Maybe it will be useful to someone.

We pay a lot of attention to prayer practice. We also try to observe certain restrictions in food. We read the Dictations and the books of the Masters.

If you carefully read and follow all that is recommended by the Masters, then the result should be manifested in two to three years. The Teaching of the Ascended Masters is the fastest Path to God.

Why are many people in the Teaching for five or six years already and do not see a significant advancement in themselves or in others? What is the reason?

The easiest way is to find the cause outside yourself. For example, it is known that the community cannot be successful if it does not include at least one Christ-being. It is also very difficult to keep the right course, not having an acting Messenger in the organization to which you belong. It is very difficult to do without a Teacher belonging to a successive chain of Guru - disciple relationships.

Yes, of course, most people need external guidelines, a compass, according to which they can verify their course.

A solo flight

Sooner or later there comes a moment on our Path when we must go by ourselves, alone. A solo flight. I now address those who are ready for the solo flight. This is a very complex segment of the Path. Not everyone is ready for it.

And one day you make a decision and rush to this dangerous section of the Path. The difficulty lies in the fact that we've already read all this hundreds of times, but here we have to really go ahead, and we do not always have the right quote from a Dictation or a friendly adviser at hand.

In fact, the only criterion is God within us. This is the most reliable adviser and the most reliable compass. But you need to get used to communicating with Him, to be able to distinguish a quiet inner voice from astral voices and your carnal mind.

How should one understand that he is ready for this dangerous part of the Path?

First of all, you need to closely monitor your thoughts and feelings. Every minute try to understand what you think and feel. If you often catch yourself on negative thoughts and feelings (you condemn someone, take offense at someone, experience some baser desires), then you are not yet ready for this section of the Path. You must wait and work with prayer.

Love literally flows out of you into the world around you

Once there is a moment of inner peace, silence, when annoying little thoughts stop jumping around like fleas, then suddenly, consciousness rises above the surrounding world and leaves behind anxiety and fear.

It is very important to realize your feelings at this moment. We are attracted to the sphere of the subtle world that we are consonant with. This state cannot be compared with anything. This is a state of complete inner peace and bliss. It seems that Love is literally pouring out of you into the world around you, and the more you give your Love, the more and more you experience the state of grace.

It is necessary to fix this state into every cell of your body, every nerve ending. The task is to learn from memory to fall into this state again and again, every day.

Actually, this is the whole secret. You get into a disharmonious situation on the street, at work, but you try to remember this state of grace and bliss. You forcibly keep your consciousness at the highest level available to you.

The difficulty is that you cannot miss a single day. At least a few minutes a day, preferably two or three hours a day, one must experience these elevated states of consciousness.

Remember your state after a good prayer, after a Dictation, after a long stay in nature or listening to classical music and reproduce this state again and again.

It helps me a lot when I'm in a state of Love. I am literally rising when I experience this feeling.

Bring your vibrations closer to the subtle worlds

I was given an exercise that helps to maintain an elevated state of consciousness throughout the day.

I imagine my I AM Presence in the form of the sun at the zenith above my head. And I imagine how I pull myself up on the rope to this sun.

When we are able to experience such states longer and longer, we bring our vibrations closer to the subtle worlds, and we can come into contact with the beings of these worlds and, above all, with our Holy Christ Self and our I AM Presence.

The criterion of the truth of such contact is our inner state. Like attracts like. We are attracted to those vibrations that our thoughts and our feelings are consonant with.

All knowledge comes from within. The most incredible things happen so naturally and simply when everything is consonant with God.

After all, I have said nothing new. We already know all of this, but for some reason did not consider it necessary to carry out.

**I love you, my readers,
And I bow before the Light of God in you.**

Give Wings to a soul[1]
Liga Zitara

I first saw the Messenger of the Great White Brotherhood, Tatyana Mickushina, in the summer of 2015, when I was invited to the Second Congress of the International social movement "THE MORALITY MOVEMENT," held in Riga. That time, Tatyana, addressing the audience, talked about her understanding of God and morality. She stood on the stage in a halo of light, strong and also really fragile, close and at the same time so far from us sitting in the dark audience. It seemed that the people held their breath so that nothing could break this sacred moment. We were catching her every word, every thought, like a fresh, thirst-quenching sip of water.

---

[1] This article was published in the Riga esoteric yearbook, "Mystery" in 2017. In the article, well-known Latvian journalist Liga Zitara from Riga with great sensitivity and tact tells of the life of Tatyana Nicholaevna Mickushina

In spring of 2016, I had the great honor to interview Tatyana Mickushina in connection with the publication of the books "The Sutras of the Ancient Teaching" and "About health, happiness, work and money" in the publishing house Sol Vita. Of course, there was the desire to understand her as a person as deeply as possible, to learn how her consciousness had been awakened so that she could receive Messages from the Teachers of Light, and how she devoted her whole life to further spread the Messages. I was gathering information bit by bit – delving into people's comments, exploring the prefaces of her books, meeting with the head of the publishing house Veronica Lace, who has cooperated with Tatyana Mickushina for many years, and returning to what I heard on the interview time and again. I realize that the facets of this person, reflected in the article, are by no means the only ones; nonetheless, they are of great significance. Dear readers, I would like to introduce you to this great person.

***

When you meet an outstanding person, there is a reverence and respect along with the uncertainty of whether you can find the right words or whether your understanding is at the same frequency with the inner essence of the person described. It's like looking at the snow-capped mountain peaks – distant and alluring, yet still elusive. The pure radiance invites and simultaneously warns that everything looks different from a distance. It is necessary to rise above, it is necessary to come closer, it is necessary to look deeper. I have risen only slightly – to the first slope where everything is still green and flowering. The wanderer still has a long way to go in order to reach the pristine, white peak.

This is the story about Tatyana Mickushina's life full of difficulties, climbing the peaks of Light.

The beginning of the Path

It all began at the age of 15, when Tatyana was in the hospital where, for several days, she was on the verge of life and death. In her school years Tatyana was an avid basketball player, frequently participating in all-Union competitions. During this time she sustained a major injury to her right elbow. A series of medical errors led to blood poisoning, and for a week doctors fought to save her life. Tatyana survived! It is exactly after the disease that her transformation began: She realized that human life is controlled by God, and therefore, she must find God. There was also another idea: She needed to learn! But she did not yet know what she was to learn.

In search of God, Tatyana began to read; her studies often went well into the early hours of the morning. She enrolled in the library and began to carefully study and outline "books about God," keeping a diary where she wrote down her reflections on life. If before Tatyana was shy to speak in front of peers, even during the answers in class, now she began to practice speaking in front of a mirror.

Later, all this came in handy for the implementation of the high Mission of Messengership.

High school was followed by five years of study at the Omsk Polytechnic Institute with a degree in design and manufacturing of electronic equipment. Tatyana graduated from the institute with honors. However, during all her years of study at the institute, she never abandoned the idea that this is not what she needs.

She worked for 13 years as a design engineer at a private factory.

"It was very hard work," said Tatyana, adding with a laugh, "I think I was trained by the Masters. It is quite possible to become a Messenger while withstanding such a load for 13 years."

Perestroika began, and with it the conversion of production. The salaries stopped coming and Tatyana had to look for another job. She worked as a chief accountant in various organizations during the following ten years. In the early 1990s, she was engaged in social and political work: She was co-chairperson of the social-ecological association "Green city," she took part in the organization of the elections, and she herself ran for the city and regional Councils of deputies in her native city of Omsk.

While all this activity did not bring Tatyana an understanding of God, her spiritual quest continued.

Approaching the Mission

At the end of 1996, Tatyana found the Teachings of the Ascended Masters given through Mark and Elizabeth Prophet, the founders of the organization "The Summit Lighthouse" in America.

Tatyana attended the events of the Russian organization that followed this Teaching and for about three years, she engaged in the reading of the decrees and performing the services.

In the year 2000, there was a person in Tatyana's life who taught her the practice of meditation. As a result of mastering this technique, Tatyana began to first communicate with her Higher Self and then to hear the Masters.

At first Tatyana asked questions and received short answers by learning to listen to thoughts sent by the Masters. She developed this gift over a period of three years.

Since November 2002, based on the proposal of the Masters, she launched an electronic edition, "Sirius" (http://sirius-ru.net), where she could share her own experience, give relevant information on spiritual topics, and give the floor to the readers.

Trials

From the moment Tatyana began to communicate with the Masters, during meditation, they worked with her on the subtle plane, with her consciousness and sub-consciousness, gradually opening her chakras. The outer shell remained the same; however, due to the finest filigree work of the Higher Beings, her subtle bodies were undergoing tremendous changes. As a result, Tatyana's well-being also experienced change, undergoing periods of pain and full prostration. Her sensitivity to noise, loud music, odors, and large crowds of people had been intensified, and all this brought a sense of discomfort. Her social circle was down to a minimum.

The culmination of tests took place at the end of 2002, from September to December. Within just a period of 4 months, Tatyana underwent the toughest trials: being fired from her job, her friends leaving her, along with not taking up any new interests. During this difficult time, she sometimes lacked the energy to walk to the kitchen to prepare meals.

But despite her poor health, Tatyana continued to meditate every day. She recalls:

"During these meditations the Masters were looking for a certain psychological state from me, the Higher State. There was something inside me that prevented me and needed to be altered or broken.

"And one day, in the presence of Lord Maitreya, I reached the state of complete humility and obedience, and I realized that if God gave life, He can take it away, and there is no death. It was a Higher State, a very subtle revelation.

"For three days, during meditation I had reached this Higher State. And then the Masters considered that the test was over, and immediately all the pain and suffering stopped."

Years later, Tatyana realized that it was during meditation that a huge amount of work had taken place and that this was the greatest work she had ever done in her life.

In the beginning, Tatyana asked the Masters a lot of questions while in the meditative state, but now she has stopped. Tatyana believes that it is pointless to ask too many silly questions because during meditation there is an intense exchange of information that alters the consciousness. As water cleans the body, washing away dirt, similarly during the meditations all the dirt is washed away from the subtle bodies and the consciousness rises. Asking the Masters questions about everyday affairs is like talking about glass when you are told about diamonds, rubies, and sapphires.

The Messenger of the Great White Brotherhood

Having passed all the tests, Tatyana obtained the right to carry out the assignment of the Masters: to represent Their interests on the physical plane. That is, Tatyana became a mediator between the upper world and humanity, the physical conductor for the transmission of the Messages to the human world.

In 2003, she was given the status of Messenger by the Masters, and the following year she was granted the Mantle of the Messenger of the Great White Brotherhood.

What is the Mantle of the Messenger? Tatyana Mickushina explains:

"It is not a merit, and it is not an order that is assigned for service. The Masters do not explain the concept of the 'Mantle' in Their Messages. I will try to explain my understanding. It is something like the credentials that the Ambassador of any country presents to the President of the country he is visiting.

"Similarly, the Masters give Their credentials, not on the physical plane but on the subtle plane. This is an energy substance, a tool that helps to hear the Masters.

"You could also say that the Mantle is a protective tool. For example, a person working with high voltage has special rubber gloves and boots for protection. In the same fashion, working with the high energies of the Masters, protective devices are also required for the person's safety. The Mantle can also be compared to a muzzle or a collar. If a person strays from the necessary course, the Masters return him."

The revelation in the Altai

In the early 1990s, Tatyana carefully read *The Secret Doctrine* by H. P. Blavatsky but the meaning of the text was not entirely understandable.

In the summer of 2004, Tatyana went to rest in Altai, in the tourist base near the village of Chemal. The Masters recommended that she take the second volume of *The Secret Doctrine* to read.

Moving away from the noise of the tourist camp, Tatyana settled on the bank of the river Katun and began to read. She found that this time she could understand the meaning of the text and filled with the joy of discovery, she continued reading until evening.

Later, after returning to Omsk, she continued to read *The Secret Doctrine* however, she was surprised to discover that, once again, she could not understand the meaning. Later, she went to a park on the opposite side of the river Irtysh, but since she was able to understand what she was reading, she made extracts from the text there. Upon returning home, she could not understand the meaning again.

Tatyana made the discovery that *The Secret Doctrine* could only be understood while at a certain energy level, in certain vibrations that could only be reached in nature with the aid of the Masters.

During her meditations, Tatyana received linking texts, which explained selected quotations from the book [*The Secret Doctrine*]. Creating a new chapter, she immediately mailed and posted the materials on the "Sirius" website.

All the material received during meditation, practically unchanged, formed the basis of the book *Good and Evil. An individual interpretation of "The Secret Doctrine" by H. P. Blavatsky*, which was written in September-October 2004.

This book has become a cornerstone, a kind of test, and admission to receive the Messages. All the conditions had been created for the writing of this book. After returning from Altai, Tatyana got fired from her job, and so she had time to write. The Masters strongly advised her to write the book and gave a great amount of energy for this.

Tatyana's consciousness had been gradually prepared. For about a year, she was told that Lucifer had been wrongly perceived by the people and that he is "not so bad," but Tatyana could not believe it. Only a year later, the Masters returned to this theme again, proposing that she read Volume II of *The Secret Doctrine* — an authoritative source for Tatyana — in the clean conditions of nature in Altai. And only when elevating her consciousness, Tatyana realized the feat of Lucifer and that Lucifer was slandered in exactly the same way as Nicholas II and Grigory Rasputin.

You must admit that the writing of a book on Lucifer, who is abused and associated with darkness by all people, and who, in fact, is "good," and the Savior of mankind, is a real feat. In the book by Tatyana Mickushina, the truth about Lucifer is brilliantly revealed, based on quotations from the book of H. P. Blavatsky.

About the receiving of the Messages

March 4, 2005, saw the occurrence of the greatest event in Tatyana's life — the day she received the first Dictation, which was not addressed to her personally but rather to all people of Earth.

The Messages were received daily for four months up until June 30; 117 Messages of the first cycle were transmitted into the world.

"It was difficult, as I live in the city center," said Tatyana.

"Receiving the Messages is a very delicate work that requires complete concentration. It is necessary to hear the inaudible and to see the invisible. After four months of continuous receiving of the Messages, I was completely exhausted. I woke up in the morning with the thought that I need to receive the Message and went to bed in the evening thinking the same. I couldn't do anything else.

"In order to receive a Message, first I enter into a meditative state and establish a connection with my Higher Self and ask which of the Masters wishes to give a Message. The Masters first wanted me to record the Messages with my voice on audio, but as soon as I heard my voice, I immediately lost the connection. Then the method changed. Now I meditate lying down until I hear the command to stand up and turn on the computer. I create a file and write down the Message and immediately, even in the presence of the Master who gave His Message, make an audio recording.

"It is exactly in the meditative state that the energy exchange occurs. This can be explained in this way: I get an impulse, like a compressed file, which is gradually being unpacked and decompressed in my consciousness. The words open exactly with the speed at which I am writing. First one word comes that needs to be written, and only then the other words follow. One day Archangel Michael came and said, 'My angels and I have come to render honors to our Messenger.' I thought it wouldn't be necessary to write this. And then nothing followed, but as soon as this phrase was written, it was followed by the next sentences.

"Interestingly, I didn't know in advance which of the Masters would come and what the subject of the Message would be."

"From the very beginning of the receiving of the Messages, I was fulfilling an important condition of the Masters: The same day when the Message is received, it must be posted on the Internet. Perhaps this condition is due to the fact that not all the Dictations through previous Messengers were published. The Masters spend a lot of energy in order to prepare the Messenger for receiving the Messages, and it is important that all the materials would reach the people. That is why, long before the receiving of the Messages, I was told to create a website under the name 'Sirius.'

"When the first cycle of Messages was received and published on the Internet, I couldn't have a rest, because I was invited to meetings. I went to Novosibirsk, then to St. Petersburg, Moscow, Altai, and Bulgaria. I was on the road all the time. There were times when I would come home for two or three weeks, and then hit the road again."

Tatyana learned from her Teacher that it would not be possible to continue receiving the Dictations in Omsk. It was necessary to find a place in nature. The readers of the site became engaged in the search.

First they found a house in Altai. Tatyana went there at the end of 2005. The house was small, without water, and with a toilet outside. She stoked the furnace. A local resident, Arthur, helped to chop and carry wood, and heated a bath.

This suggests that the screening and tests continued. Tatyana knew that she must withstand; she accepted any difficulties as the norm. It was heroism, which she is not going to admit, and endurance, which was developed in adolescence. All difficulties can be overcome if the true Path is found.

The following three cycles of the Messages (3rd, 4th, and 5th) were received in Moscow, in Bulgaria, and in the Vladimir region.

But in the summer of 2007, the following cycles were received in the Ashram near Omsk. A total of 10 cycles were received there (6th to 15th), from June 2007 to January 2012.

A Threat

Certainly, the area where the Messages are received is filled by the Masters with the powerful energy of Light, which the outer world begins to resist, trying to return the level of vibrations back to the usual state. This is expressed through the people who are beginning to resist the new state of affairs and strike over and over.

Tatyana Mickushina built a house not far from Omsk. Then, thanks to the donations of people, a Training Center was also built near the house.

The Training Center was built by volunteers, who appeared immediately after the announcement on the Internet, as well as people who understood construction. Tatyana herself had followed the construction progress. The three-story building was built in record time: six months.

Soon after, the man who sold Tatyana the land wanted to take back his former property. The court proceedings lasted from December 2008 for almost 3 years, in different instances, including the Supreme Court of Russia. In the wake of the long court proceedings, about 60 hectares had been lost, which is about 1/3 of the purchased land, leaving 100 hectares. It took over a year to recover the documents of land ownership, which mysteriously disappeared from justice.

The very next day, on April 19, 2012, after all documents had been restored, there was a fire, similar to an assassination attempt.

On that day, Tatyana was returning from the Training Center to her house, where her assistant and associate, Tatyana, was waiting for her. Everything was very quiet. There were no people, no smell of smoke — there were no signs of the tragedy. After arriving at the house, Tatyana heard a strange hissing sound. Looking out of the window, she found that 10-15 meters of wooden fence was on fire with flames rising to a height of more than 4 meters. A fire of such power couldn't flare up in a matter of minutes, because the fence was treated with fire retardant liquid. There was no doubt that it was arson when the fire immediately surrounded all four sides of the inside of the fenced area. People, running from the Training Center, tried to extinguish the fire together with Tatyana, five of them working to defend the bathhouse. The fire spread from the fence, making its way through the grass, and it quickly reached the pines and birches (including those planted near the house) and was underway at a height of 15 meters. The fire was coming from all sides, and people locked themselves in the house, which was gradually being filled with smoke. The siding on the roof, under which there was foam insulation — a highly combustible material — began to melt and snap.

Tatyana called upon Archangel Michael to help: "Archangel Michael, help me, help me, help me!" After strongly shouting this call in space several times, there was silence. The fire, raging outside, went away. The burning pine, whose branches touched the roof, settled down to a height of 2 meters.

The firefighters arrived and extinguished the remaining flames, and after some time people could go outside. The MES officer, after a long time, prepared a report, but the cause of the fire was not determined.

On July 19, the same year, there was a second fire, this time near the Training Center. Following these events, people from around the world began to write letters addressing the President of Russia with a request to investigate and protect Tatyana. The petition was signed by more than 3,500 people, which led to the arrival of the lieutenant-colonel of police; however, this did not help.

Following this series of events, the Masters themselves decided to protect their Messenger: The next six cycles of the Messages were no longer received in Russia.

As always, God acts through people. On hearing this news, the director of the publishing house Sol Vita, Veronica Lace, invited the Messenger to Latvia to help Tatyana recover from the fire.

"When the information of this unfortunate event appeared on the Internet, I immediately called Tatyana and invited her to come to Latvia. She doubted that this was possible, as an ordinary visa has a waiting period of about a month," said Veronica Lace. "I promised to arrange that, and miraculously the visa was obtained within a period of three days. We also quickly found a wonderful place outside Kuldīga, in the middle of the forest — a newly built and still uninhabited house, without other people's energies. This is an example of how the Higher Power acts. When you make the right choice, everything is arranged without undue effort."

Only this Path makes sense

Receiving the Messages from the Beings of Light, Teachers of mankind, Tatyana is spreading the Divine Wisdom and laying the foundation for philosophical and ethical Teaching that is based on the Highest Moral Law, the Law of Karma and the Law of Reincarnation. The last Law is very important because it reveals the eternal, undying part of a person. When a person realizes that he lives not one life but many lives and that all his current thoughts, feelings and actions determine his immediate and distant future, he begins to live life more consciously and responsibly, controlling his reactions to events.

During the period 2005 to 2015, Tatyana Mickushina received more than 470 Messages, published in a series of books *Words of Wisdom*, and published in the Latvian language by Sol Vita.

The Messages highlight the necessity of the changing of people's consciousness and finding a new meaning of life. The Messages help to overcome hopelessness, restore vitality, and lift one's spirits. This is evidenced by the admiring reviews that Tatyana Mickushina receives after the release of each new book.

"I have been reading the books by Tatyana Mickushina for the second year, and they have helped me to strengthen all aspects of my life. I feel a sense of joy and peace that I had never experienced before. It is enough to read even a line from a Message or a Rosary that the mood and the world perception will improve. I no longer feel like a victim at work, and I ceased to be affected by self-pity. I have learned to cooperate with the director and colleagues. I am deeply grateful to the Messenger Tatyana Mickushina who made this Teaching available to the whole world."

Grant Vospher,
Los Angeles, CA, USA

"The author of the book 'Good and Evil' read 'The Secret Doctrine' by H. P. Blavatsky from a new angle, and I express my gratitude to her for that. Because people with an open view of the world can give a new impulse to the consciousness and a new impulse of thought, in which one can come to such unexpected and paradoxical conclusions that inspire and delight the soul."

Elena Ilyina,
writer, Russia

"I was in severe depression when my friend gave me the book 'Words of Wisdom' by Tatyana Mickushina, which contains Messages of the Teachers of the world. We read the Messages with her, then we read the Rosary of Mother Mary; we fasted and prayed. We were completely isolated from society for two weeks. It was a deep immersion into the vibrations of the Divine world. And then a miracle happened — a complete transformation! I felt a burst of strength, energy, and creativity. There was a force of life. There was a reassessment — I was born again. My gratitude has no end!!! I send my regards and infinite admiration. This is truly the Divine Teaching, which gives a modern man the chance to live in this world and receive the joy of fellowship and the

joy of love, harmony, and integrity. This Teaching gives a chance to understand that only with God all things are possible!" With gratitude and love,

Donna Luna, Venice, Italy

"The books by Tatyana Mickushina give wings to our souls, and remind us of the supreme goal of our life. They are the Divine nectar the soul yearns for; and, having tasted that, we don't want to eat what the mass media feed us.

"From the preface to the book
"The life-changing Wisdom!"

I live surrounded by Light

The lives of the people who communicate with Tatyana Mickushina over a long period of time, irrevocably change — for the better, of course; although perhaps, it may not seem so at first glance. Priorities, life perceptions, and the environment all change. New people enter our lives.

These are the changes that happened to Veronica Lace:

"First of all, I began to treat myself with greater responsibility because I have to be aware of every one of my words and actions; I have to control my feelings and my attitude towards each person and every aspect of life. This wisdom has become an integral part of my life. At first, I was in great awe of Tatyana Mickushina, and after closer acquaintance, there appeared a deep respect."

"The further it is, the harder and more serious everything becomes. All events and all circumstances of life are perceived in a new way. At first I thought about what I could do to help the Messenger. And now, I publish books.

"After meeting the Messenger, I realized that the main thing is still to come, and much more needs to be done.

"Someday communities will be created where intelligent and gifted children — the God-men who will not be in contact with violence — can be born. And within 25-50 years they will change the world. I foresee the appearance of the communities of light-minded people all over the world. People will read more and their thoughts will become natural and easy. And this way of life will become crucial.

"In my life, I have met many outstanding people whom I was fortunate enough to be around. However, what I feel in the presence of the Messenger is indescribable. I am grateful to God for this opportunity.

"In her presence, one cannot fail to do good, and neither be dishonest or unable.

"I have an understanding of the universal principles of creation. Before that, I respected all religions, every search for God, and venerated the holy but have only now realized essentially what Divinity and God is.

"God is not an old man with a beard, as He exists in the minds of many. And, unfortunately, science does not give any explanation. The Masters want us to evolve and reach the Divine heights. For this, we need to cope with our 'demons'; lust, the desire for pleasure, the manifestation of ego and other negative states of consciousness. Hell exists not somewhere else, but on the Earth; whether we like it or not, daily we come in contact with it on different levels. One can see this only when he understands that the consciousness of society is degraded.

"The seminars of Tatyana Mickushina, in which she explains the essence of the Ancient Teaching and the essence of the work on oneself, were very valuable for me. I truly realized that, only when I started to know God within myself, within my heart. This is not easy to understand without knowledge of the Teaching that the Masters transmitted through Tatyana, although there are a lot of books filled with the unnecessary mental difficulties and limitations of their authors.

"I came to the conclusion that I have not met another responsible person like Tatyana in my life. If she gives her word, then it will be so. She trusts people completely, not recognizing suspicion or doubt. At the same time, she feels if there is something wrong. Now I am capable of exercising greater discernment.

"My social circle has significantly changed; my living environment has changed but I have only noticed these things over the course of time. I live in another circle," assures Veronica Lace.

* * *

This circle of Light includes everyone who is studying the Messages and notes the changes brought about by this philosophical and ethical Teaching that comes into our lives, thanks to Tatyana Mickushina. All of us are travelers, climbing the mountain; we strive for the summit, the radiant heights, shining bright in the sun, where the Teachers of Light, surrounded by the Messengers of the Great White Brotherhood are encouraging Their followers: "Keep going, the climb is worth it!"

***

*How can each of us find this Path?
Where does it lie? Can we reach the top
of the luminous Peaks alone?
What is the Path — the Path to the Light?*

Internal and external Path

T. N. Mickushina

Mankind has always, at all times sought to know the Truth through a variety of methods: be it science, art, or religion. There are many people who in the process of knowing the truth have achieved more progress than those around them. They founded their own schools, religions, or philosophical systems. Other people choose to follow one or another external dogma, the external system. The founder of one system, ideology or religion sought to convey the truth to his followers and disciples as he understood it.

But you must admit that any manmade philosophical system, belief, or religion is restricted at least by reason of the limitations inherent in the human consciousness. How can one describe the Infinite God, the scheme of the Universe, with a reliable degree of accuracy, having at his disposal imperfect tools? This process could be compared to trying to measure the distance between the nucleus and electrons in the atom with an ordinary student ruler.

Human development takes place through the expansion of consciousness

Our consciousness is limited. The development of mankind occurs through the expansion of consciousness. In this process some are more successful than others. The only difference between us and the Ascended Masters is the level of consciousness.

In other words, we can say that the only difference between God and us is the level of consciousness.

The level of our consciousness is related to our vibrations; in other words, it can be said that the level of our consciousness is related to karma. After all, what is Karma? We know that karma is misused energy that is deposited in our electronic belt as "viscous treacle." This energy binds us to the material world in which we live because this energy is in consonance with the world around us.

The greatest sages and philosophers of all time achieved their insights precisely because their vibrations differed in their level from the vibrations of most people. This allowed their consciousness to reach great heights from which they drew their knowledge.

How to ease your Path, support tools

Any dogma or restriction by an external religion, established by its founders, is aimed only at being a sign, a reminder of what needs to be done to make the Path easier.

Thou shalt not kill ... Thou shalt not steal ... Do not commit adultery ... Observe the fast ... Pray ...

In and of themselves these restrictions are not a panacea, rather they are as supporting means to ease the Path and throw off the fetters of this world, the imperfect energies that bind us to the earth, lifetime after lifetime.

And if we are successful in our efforts, our consciousness soars up, and we do not see the world as if through a muddy glass. We see things as they are.

Followers of Christ, Buddha, and others, (those who did not possess or do not have an expanded Christ consciousness,) tend to focus on external dogmas and limitations, forgetting why they are needed.

This is just as if we were carefully preparing to go on the road, taking with us all the necessary things — a supply of water, food, saddled our horses — and set out on the Path. The only thing that we did not do is define the purpose of our journey, and consequently we do not know in which direction to go. But we have set out.

If we do not set ourselves the goals that God wants us to reach, our movement would be meaningless. Yes, we will comply with all praying, restrictions on food and the rules of conduct, but — why?

What God wants from us

We We know that the New Epoch, the Age of Aquarius, has come. New energies came to Earth. Our consciousness has even more opportunities for development. Maybe something has to change in our purposes?

How do we know what has changed? It is not on the radio or on television and it is unlikely that we can read about it in the newspapers.

God has always sent His Messengers and Prophets to enable people to obtain the necessary information through them. But who are the Messengers and Prophets? These are people who, thanks to their past achievements and newly acquired skills, have developed the ability to hear the voice of God, to understand His language.

This can be achieved by everyone.

Why do we so often focus on limitations and dogmas and why do we so rarely think about what God really wants from us?

God wants us to return Home, to Him. To do that we must give up, surrender, every part of our mortal selves. This is just a different level of consciousness that is available to all of us, right now. We just need to abandon dogmas and strive to God.

We just need to be aware every moment of our lives that the physical body is given to us temporarily. It is simply an instrument of God, required for Him to act in the physical world. It is not our body, it belongs to God. We must always remember this.

Our emotional body also belongs to God. We must surrender voluntarily our human feelings to God. Then more and more often we will experience Divine feelings. We will be able to feel unconditional, Divine Love.

We must also turn away from our mental and etheric bodies, from our human thoughts and aspirations. Then God can work through us.

The quality of Love is action

Yes, prayers are needed; they transform the subtle worlds and their action sooner or later affects our physical world. But we need concrete action on the physical plane.

The ability to act and interact is a manifestation of the quality of Love on the physical plane.

Whatever anyone may tell me about his achievements, or his ability to communicate with the Masters, I see the level of achievement of a person reflected in his ability to act. The ability to do the work of God in the physical octave indicates a high level of human achievement. But only to do exactly what God wants to be done, and not what we think God wants to be done. There is a difference.

We are here to do the work of God. We are here to realize our Being, to be God in embodiment.

How to determine our consonance with the world of God

Of course in Their time, Jesus and Buddha, along with others, have already told mankind everything that was needed. But God continues to send His Messengers and Prophets. Why? Because the illusion of this world is strong, because we need tuning forks by which we can determine our consonance with the world of God.

Someone can achieve everything himself, using only books and lectures, but I'm sure that there is something that is transmitted in addition to books from the Teacher's aura to the disciple's aura. Only in direct communication can a full exchange of energy be possible, allowing us to rise to a new level of consciousness and to accelerate and increase our vibrations. This reduces the travel time in one life — that is, of course, as long as we make the right choices.

Finding God within

Our world is dual. In every religion, in every church, there are people who choose an external path, the path of church dogmas and a church career. By and large this is the path of the world, leading to death.

And in every faith and religion, there are also people who opt for the inner Path, to seek and find God within themselves and to become God in embodiment. Any church is strong precisely because of these people. And the wise leadership of the external church will never persecute these people because it gains its strength through them. For example, in the Orthodox Church this strength comes from the elders and Saints, such as Saint Sergius of Radonezh and Saint Seraphim of Sarov in Russia. Surely there are such people now, and they can be found almost at every service, in almost every church.

I outlined my thoughts about God. And I think it will help you, my readers, to better understand me and my aspirations.

With all my Love to you,
Tatyana Mickushina

From conversations with the Messenger

To live according to the Teaching of the Masters of Wisdom

Currently, the Masters of Wisdom have given a complete Teaching.

This Teaching is contained in the books "Words of Wisdom" and in more than 60 different books created according to the Teaching and Messages.

This Teaching contains a program for changing the whole society that exists on planet Earth so that this society can conform to the Divine Principles. But in order for society to be able to restructure itself in accordance with the Divine Principles, a critical mass of people in that society must adopt these Principles and live in accordance with them.

According to the Masters of Wisdom, for society to see positive development, it is necessary that one percent of the population assimilate the Teaching of the Masters. In Russia this is about 1.5 million people, and in the world it is about 60 million people.

Therefore, if a country like Russia adopts the Moral Law, the Cosmic Law of this Universe, then changes in all the other countries would occur more rapidly.

The purpose of the Messages of the Masters is to encourage people to turn toward God and begin to follow the Moral or Divine Law that exists in the Universe.

By and large, all the major religions and teachings aim to ensure that people adhere to some moral principles.

If you take any sacred books, they all say the same thing — maybe it's written in different words, but the meaning is the same.

There is something called the "living bearer of knowledge." When we simply read, we do not believe that this applies to us personally and should be applied in our lives.

However, when a person appears who does not just read books but lives as it is written in books, it encourages other people to do the same.

Our task now is to apply this Teaching in practice.

You yourself can try to establish an inner communication with your Higher Self and the Masters, and it will be similar to making fire by the friction of rubbing two sticks together.

Or you can go to a fire which is already burning and ignite your lamp. However, once you've lit your lamp, you are responsible for keeping the flame burning by yourself.

Each of us is a particle of God

All the people who live on planet Earth are at different levels of consciousness. Understanding God will therefore vary and rely on the level of consciousness of the individual.

There is a level of consciousness that needs guardianship and external guidance. For a person at this level, it would be right to understand the concept of God within the framework of the religion to which his family or clan belongs.

However, as man develops, the concept of "God" becomes more common for him, more common than any religious dogma or idea. And man begins to realize that maybe God is a few centimeters under the palm, which is superimposed on the area of the heart.

The next level of understanding God, for man, is when he begins to realize that he is the cell of a vast organism that is the whole manifest and non-manifest Universe. The whole Universe is the body of God and each of us a very small, small particle of God.

This understanding of God is confirmed by modern science.

Modern science in its advanced areas, including quantum physics, has come to realize that there is a common Law that governs everything that happens in this Universe and that everything is interconnected with everything. That is, all of us are on some level closely connected with each other and with the whole Universe.

Our relationship with God

Our relationship with God is the main issue that we need to address, if not in this, then in subsequent lives — no matter how much we try to delay the resolution of this issue. Moreover, it is a very personal question, which is decided by each individual and not necessarily as part of a particular religion or belief.

We must constantly remember God and be guided by the highest motive available to us in all life situations.

Even if our choices bring apparent harm at the level of our lower, human part, these choices should be true in terms of our Higher, Divine part.

To achieve this in life you must understand yourself. Knowledge is given by the Masters but Knowledge must be applied individually.

Whatever we do in our life, we must do it with the right motive, out of a sense of duty to our children, to our parents, to our homeland, to our friends. When we do something out of duty, we are actually doing Karma-yoga. That is, we dedicate all that we do to God.

It is best to speak with God in the language of the heart, completely disconnecting the outer mind and vocabulary. When we speak to God through the physical features of the brain, we are willy-nilly connecting our ego along with its imperfections. Sometimes prayer simply takes the form of a deal with God: I give you the energy of prayer, and you give me health, money, etc.

When we disable the outer mind and begin to speak in the language of the heart, we just give God our Love, our Gratitude, asking nothing in return.

Our hearts know that God knows best what to send us: health or infirmity, wealth or poverty, a throne or a block. God knows better than we do what is necessary for us to become worthy to behold the glory of the Lord.

It is impossible to enter into the Kingdom of God on the shoulders of another person.

To be of the Holy Spirit is possible only by applying personal efforts tirelessly on a daily basis. There are no weekends, holidays, or vacations in spiritual work.

The whole world needs our Love

Everything around us is energy and vibration. We also bear vibrations. On the subtle plane, on the plane of emotions and thoughts, we are giant generators. We can either direct perfect or imperfect energies into the world; therefore, each of us is constantly having an effect on the whole world.

Our physical world, Earth, is sick; she needs medicine, and the best medicine for her as well as for each of us is Love.

The whole world needs our Love.

The feeling of Love should come from the heart. It either is or is not. But when we are in tune with God, feelings of Love, Compassion, and Mercy are with us, even for a little while, even for a few minutes a day.

True Love is unconditional; this is an internal quality of Love. If a man is able to experience true Love, then he automatically enters the Divine state of consciousness.

One can get acquainted with a variety of teachings that exist in this world and absorb them over a period of one incarnation, two incarnations, a hundred incarnations, a thousand incarnations...

Or one can just Love. By having this one quality, one automatically gains access to the Universal Bank of knowledge and information.

When people live for each other, they are happy

The spiritual component, the inner Moral Law, inherent and intrinsic in all people, determines life in all other spheres: politics, economics, science and education, etc.

However, if the majority of people do not accept the Moral Law (and the Messages of the

Ascended Masters are nothing more than an explanation, first of all, of the Moral Law and its inseparable connection with the Law of Karma), then such people can only be governed from the position of power and totalitarianism because there is no internal ruler in man — conscience.

Civilized, wise people, as opposed to uncivilized and unwise people, are able to agree and negotiate among themselves. On the basis of dialogue and discussion we can find common ground, a common position, ideology and general direction of movement and we thereby determine the future.

We have to try and find out what we have in common. When we find what we have in common, then we are able to negotiate and agree.

What do we have in common? The common thing between us is that we are all human beings. We are all human beings living on planet Earth in those conditions that currently exist. We must build on this outlook by looking for those things we have in common that can unite us and by directing our energies to Unity rather than division.

Then, when people have within themselves solid moral and ethical foundations, a firm belief in Divine Principles and Divine Guidance, these people are able to maintain the balance around the globe with the help of their inner strength, faith, conviction, and love that they have for all Creation.

It is this love and faith that underpins the whole society. When people live for each other, then they are happy.

We must return to God

In our society, all the major problems are associated with the fact that we have simply stopped paying attention to God. All of our problems have arisen because of this.

By and large, in the world we live in, there are only two fundamental ideologies.

One ideology is that of the consumerist society, which is currently prevailing in the world. The second ideology is the Divine ideology.

There is not a single party, politician, or country in the world that advocates the Divine world view and Divine Law. Not one country or party in the world!

The world that sees itself as being apart from God is doomed to extinction. It is like a cancer that affects humans. If this tumor is not removed in time, it will take all the reserves of the organism, and the body will die.

The same goes for our consumerist society, which lives only in order to get, get, and get pleasure, pleasure, and more pleasure from this life. Our parasitic society is like a cancer. In this type of society everything is done to stop people from thinking about God.

Just as there are two ideologies, that of the consumerist society and that of the Divine, there are also two kinds of people in our society: those who believe in God and those who do not.

Those people who do not believe in God think that this life is the only one. For them there is no Law of Karma, Law of Reincarnation, or Moral Law. They are allowed to take everything they need in life, everything that is possible, including all the pleasures and delights of this life, regardless of how these pleasures are obtained: by theft, lies, slander or other means.

Society has ceased to control all areas of human activity: advertising, music, art, books, movies, education, health, and food production.

People do not understand what is happening and how this affects the death of the human soul.

Over time many religions have removed the Law of Karma and the Law of Reincarnation.

As we live in a dual world, there is a confrontation, a struggle between two forces: the forces of good and the forces of evil. Somehow the opposing forces have tried to bury and delete the concept of the Law of Karma in many religions. Why was this necessary?

If, in our minds, we are not aware of the fact that all of our actions in this world have consequences and that we will have to face these consequences either in this life or the next, then everything is allowed.

Then we can kill, steal, lie, and no retribution will follow.

But why was it necessary to remove the Law of Reincarnation? If we have no understanding that we are not just living one life but many, that we will have other lives ahead of us, then what's the point of being careful and respectful toward nature? What's the point of doing good? You just need to take everything from life, to have fun.

Everything is always determined in this world by the best representatives of humanity.

I hope that each of us will do everything in his power to give life to this world.

I invite you to Labor Day!

T. N. Mickushina's address to followers of the Teaching of the Masters of Wisdom

Thanks to the latest scientific discoveries in the field of brain research, it became clear why mankind has stalled and sidetracked on the road of evolution.

Everything relies on our attitude towards Labor

Then, when there is no aspiring action on the physical plane, when labor is only a source of obtaining a means of subsistence, when the nature of labor is changed and distorted beyond recognition, when labor has ceased to be of a Sacred character, mankind has ceased to develop in accordance with the evolutionary law taught to us by the Masters.

The work of a human in the physical world has turned *from a way of existence* to *a means of existence*, which is one of the biggest distortions of the Divine Law existing in our Universe.

Attachments and dependencies have replaced real Labor

If there is no quality in the process of labor on the physical plane, then there is no formation of neural connections in the brain necessary for human development.

Therefore, a person seeks on the physical plane substitutes, surrogates, which constantly stimulate certain parts of the brain that must be developed during the incarnation.

Thus various attachments and dependencies are acquired: drug, alcohol, tobacco, attachment to rock music, and others.

As the world becomes more subtle, more subtle forms of dependency are acquired.

For example, when people do not apply the Teaching given by the Masters, in practice, they are forced to continually stimulate those parts of the brain that need to be developed.

These people constantly require more and more energy to recharge. They are always looking for more dictations, seminars and information. They move from one teaching to another, looking for pleasures, for a holiday, but they cannot find satisfaction anywhere because they have strayed from the evolutionary Path of development.

Such people can only be helped by allowing them to experience real quality work, which is aimed at the Common Good.

To show the world selfless Labor for the Common Good

The Masters call under Their banners those who are ready to show the world selfless Labor for the Common Good. The most effective way of spreading the Teaching is through personal example and the organization of work on the physical plane in accordance with the Principles given by the Masters. The representatives of the opposing forces are well aware of this. It is precisely due to this reason that there is enhanced resistance that is associated with the implementation of concrete work in the physical plane.

It does not even matter what we do. What's important is the demonstration of a new attitude toward Labor. It is important to establish new principles of relationships based on the Moral Laws, cooperation, mutual help, and Love.

A lot of people read the Dictations that are given by the Masters through me. Fewer people read Rosaries. Many people are willing to participate in the seminars. And only a few are willing to perform selfless Work for the Common Good. And a fraction of those few are willing to devote their lives to the Cause of the Masters.

I invite you to the Celebration of Labor! Those who wish to get to the celebration of life — We are going with a different direction on this.

Tatyana Mickushina
Light and Love!

We must return to God!
O. A. Ivanova

Constantly reading the "Sirius" newsletters and rereading the articles by T. N. Mickushina, I never cease to be amazed, not so much by the depth of the materials as their extraordinary heights: Every thought, every sentence is as though it was sent to us from Heaven. You feel those heights, and aspire to them daily with every deed and every thought. This is all the more difficult when there is no one to lead you by the hand and every choice has to be made individually. But at least now there is a landmark, a lighthouse, by which you can always check your course. This is the Messenger, T. N. Mickushina. Tatyana Nicholaevna calls herself a "pointer in the swamp of our life," showing the Path to the Peak of the Divine Consciousness. "There is the Peak of the Divine Consciousness, and I know how to get to there. Just believe in God and the Masters, and consistently move toward the Peak every day," she says to her followers. The example is her very life, every day of which is completely dedicated to serving God and the people.

T. N. Mickushina is a great worker as evidenced by the number of written and published books, regularly updated "Sirius" website, constant meetings, interviews, and conversations with followers of the Teaching.

The main objective of the Messenger is to spread the Teaching of the Masters of Wisdom as much as possible on Earth. She does not tolerate slackers around her who are arguing over what the best way to do something is but all the while are doing nothing.

Therefore, every person who has volunteered to help her is loaded with work to the limit. Here you will not sit in sweet contemplation: She supervises the work and asks about the results because she is the Messenger of Heaven, her time on Earth is short, and one has to do everything that has been entrusted. That is why Tatyana Nicholaevna treats other people with the same exactitude as she treats herself, and when one of the assistants needs to be "corrected" on the Path, then, as they say, "to the fullest" — that is, from "storm" to "thunderstorm." It can be difficult not to be offended, not to get mad, not to be outraged, but to understand that it is said by a Teacher who cares profoundly for the "scolded" person, and that perhaps she herself suffers even more from having to bring up such a topic. How else does one help a person to get rid of all the unnecessary accumulated baggage that prevents him from reaching the Peak? It is necessary to be direct and say sharp things, to "work like sandpaper" to clear away everything disturbing our growth. It happens that someone can't stand it and moves, whether to another teaching, religion, or "simply to live."

She always remembers and waits for this person to return to the Path. She remembers everyone and is waiting because she loves each of us with unconditional Love coming from God. She is always surprised when we do not cooperate, disagree, or quarrel with each other. "Why don't you love each other? We are all parts of God! We are One." For her, it's as natural as breathing.

Tatyana Nicholaevna is a very cheerful person; she is almost always smiling. And when she laughs (mostly over us, over our ignorance), it is impossible to resist, and you begin to laugh at yourself with her. She can present any "training" situation of our life with such humor and so artistically that it will be remembered forever, and you try the next time (if the situation ever happens again), not to look like a "monkey," "crow," or "sheep." Her smile and sense of humor are very helpful in listening to her and communicating with her, like with a wise man who in any situation reveals the Divine Path.

For nearly 15 years, T. N. Mickushina has taught those who can and want to hear her, always repeating the same thing, "You must go back to God!" And at some point you begin to understand what she wants us to do. Most importantly, what you begin to understand is that it is not she, as a person, but rather God who speaks through her to us and you begin to take her every word with a completely different meaning.

At the beginning of the Path Tatyana Nicholaevna has said, "It is necessary to absorb the Teaching of the Masters and live with the Teaching." It takes more than one year. But when you start to "absorb" the Teaching, completely unnoticed your whole life begins to change. Absolutely everything changes: friends, habits, and your attitude to everything.

You begin to build not only this life in which you live but also you are already thinking about the next, to "program" it.

And perhaps, one of the most important achievements is the understanding that you can change the life you have lived by changing your attitude toward the events of that life. Tatyana Nicholaevna helps to rewrite life and this is quite extraordinary.

From her Faith in God, devotion to the Masters of the Great White Brotherhood, and Love for humanity she draws her courage and infinite patience to stand alone against all attacks, ignorance, unbelief, pride, egotism, aggression... the list of our anti-virtues can be very long. Even one man in the field is a Warrior if he is with God!

Before any work, the Messenger T. N. Mickushina tells us, "With God," not letting us stay alone. You get used to saying it yourself, when you wake up and throughout the whole day you say it to each person nearby, and mentally wish it to everyone you want to help.

WITH GOD!

BOOKS BY
TATYANA N. MICKUSHINA

MASTERS OF WISDOM SERIES

Each of the Masters of Wisdom strives to give us what they consider most vital at the present moment of transition. Every message contains the energies of different Masters who give those messages. The Masters speak about the current historical moment on planet Earth. They tell us about energy and vibrations, about the illusion of this world and about the Divine Reality, about the Higher Self of a human and about his lower bodies. They give us concrete recommendations on exactly how to change our own consciousness and continue on the evolutionary Path. It is recommended that you prepare yourself for reading every message very carefully. You have to tune to the Master who is giving the message with the help of proper music, with the help of the Master's image, or by using a prayer or a meditation before reading the Message. That way you align your energies, elevate your consciousness, and the messages can benefit you.

SAINT GERMAIN

Saint Germain is at present an Ascended Master, the Hierarch of the New Age. In his last incarnation as the Count de Saint Germain in the 18th century, he exerted a great influence on the course of world history. The Messages of Master Saint Germain are charged with optimism and faith in the forthcoming Golden Age! He teaches about preparing for a New Age by transforming our consciousness, and reminds us: "Joy and Love come to you when your Faith is steadfast, when you rely in your consciousness on God and the Ascended Hosts."

SANAT KUMARA

Masters of Wisdom, first of all Sanat Kumara, remind us about our Divine origin and call us to wake up to a Higher reality, because Divine Reality by its love, wisdom, and beauty exceeds any of the most wonderful aspects of our physical world. The Messages of Sanat Kumara include Teachings on true and false messengers, Communities of the Holy Spirit, responsibility for the duties that one has taken upon him/herself before their incarnation, the right use of the money energy, the choice of everyone between the Eternal and the perishable world, overcoming the ego, the Path of Initiations, and many other topics.

MORYA

Messages from the Teacher, Master Morya, have been given through Helena Blavatsky in the 19th century, Helena and Nicholas Roerich in the period around 1920-1950, and Mark and Elizabeth Clare Prophet in the 1960's. Master Morya is still actively working on the Spiritual plane to help the humanity of the World. Now the Masters continue their work through a Messenger from Russia, Tatyana Mickushina.

This book contains selected Messages from Master Morya. Many Teachings are given in the

Messages, including the Teachings about the correct actions on the physical plane, Service to Brotherhood, the attainment of the qualities of a disciple such as devotion, persistence, aspiration, and discipline. Some aspects of the Teaching about changing of consciousness are also introduced here.

SHIVA

The present volume contains selected Messages of Lord Shva. Many Teachings are given in these Messages; including the Teaching about God, the Teaching about Discernment of reality from illusion: which helps to ascend to a new level of consciousness and also new aspects of the Guru-chela relationship are considered.

Author page of T. N. Mickushina on Amazon:
amazon.com/author/tatyana_mickushina

THE MESSENGER

Author-compiler O. A. Ivanova

Translator: Julia Zaitseva

Please, leave your review about this book at amazon.com. This will greatly help in spreading the Teaching of the Ascended Masters given through the Messenger Tatyana Mickushina.

Websites:

http://sirius-eng.net (English version)
http://sirius-ru.net (Russian version)

Books by T.N.Mickushina on amazon.com:
amazon.com/author/tatyana_mickushina

Made in the USA
Columbia, SC
13 November 2023